Surrendering to the Path

44 New Poems

44 Selected Poems

by

Robert Eugene Perry

Dig your stuff
brother! :)

Surrendering to the Path

Everyone has a path.

All of us want to belong somewhere, to find that place we can call home. Each of us seeks a connection with each other, and with something larger than ourselves.

The truth is that we are all connected. The fate of each of us is in the hands of us all. Seeking authenticity, we long to leave behind the labels that divide us.

I consider myself a metaphysical poet. I attempt to draw out the divine to illumine the mundane. It is a matter of perception. There is really nothing that is just ordinary in life. Everything is miraculous.

I feel the poet's calling is to reveal the sublime truth of the world around us by engaging it fully, and attempting to reveal its essence by way of symbol and metaphor.

The Divine Third

and

Snow Drifts

Published in

Mizmor Poetry Anthology, 2020

Published by Human Error Publishing
www.humanerrorpublishing.com
paul@humanerrorpublishing.com

Copyright © 2020
by
Human Error Publishing
&
Robert Eugene Perry

All Rights Reserved

ISBN#: 978-1-948521-41-3

Cover design
by
Paul Richmond
and
Robert Eugene Perry

Dedication

To my beloved, Kristina, who has always encouraged my spiritual exploration. For my sons Joshua and Zachary, who have taught me that I am not nearly as smart as I think I am. For my spiritual companions who have travelled with me in this journey, you have taught me a measure of humility. I thank you all.

44 New Poems

44 Selected Poems

A Seed Which Changes Everything

When I was young
I went on an adventure
in the woods behind my home.

The memory of it is surreal and dreamlike,
the familiar woods transformed
into another realm.

Walking through the forest
along the well-worn path, something
urged me into a grove of sumacs.

Pushing through
I came to a small clearing
full of light.

I have spent years trying to recall exactly what happened,
have dreamed of this place,
and can still see it vividly.

Returning to the area I have found the sumacs, but
not the clearing. Something otherworldly and inexplicable occurred.
I have never been the same.

Some days I wish I could remember the event,
but I have a suspicion that it retains its power
because of the mystery it presents.

Creator sometimes acts like a secret agent,
infiltrating the ordinary to plant a sacred seed
which changes
everything.

After the Rain/ End of Day

trees move
leaves twist

reflecting bits
of sunlight

after the rain
comes the dance

a dendrophiliac's
delight.

======

the last golden rays of the day
reveal the longing in my soul
they whisper: more than this,
more than this visible arena.

twilight creeps in, shadows deepen
exposing the agony of letting go –
speak of dying, of sloughing off
emerging as something other.

clouds spread their fingers to
part the blue, shades of red
bleed into the sky making way
for the dark canopy of night.

Exploration of Existence as Such

I. wintertide

Winter came, and with it thoughts of desolation.
the snow, the ice, the heavy dull clouds
all whispered that the world was dead,
the sun only a myth of days past, long ago
when we were young and virile
parks were green, children played
and the only cold came
from ice cream cones
greedily devoured
before they
melted.

A single gull in the sky,
white against the gray
a paean to wintertide,
and those who've lost their way.

II. calling

Blind old man with second sight
      told of future days to pass
held the Fool up to the light
      the Cards upon the table cast
young man took the Fool and left
      a journey called his eager heart
the seer saw his last request
      and begged the angels to depart.

III. beginning

The bloom of love
once planted, supersedes
all other thoughts,

all other needs.

> Mystical dawn, primordial fire
> the ancients worshiped well and knew
> all life depends upon that circle
> warmth, light, consistency; epiphany
> called the dawning of awareness,
> and awareness the beginning of
> life anew.

At the edge of the precipice, staff in hand
eyes towards golden sunlit strands
the Fool begins his holy quest
steps off, and flies above the rest.

IV. desert

Sirocco wind and scorching sun
> swirling sands and scorpions

barren tract of desert waste
> yet everything is in its place

Forty days without a bite
> burning days and freezing nights

looking for the inner light
> that will put the world to rights

V. illumination

Equanimity a lofty goal on a noble path
the fruit of right living plucked from a tree in perfect season
at just the right moment.

Each instant becomes the new movement
over and again until we see it
for what it truly is.

You can step in the River, but it is never the same twice
is it the River that changes
or is it you?

Aspirations

The sound of my own voice,
hollow and distant,
cannot express
this heart
yearning to awaken from listlessness,
seeking the connectedness of all things;
all things working together, reaching
skyward towards the creator,
the sustainer,
the liberator.

All creation groans under
the astounding weight of the ages.
Decay and entropy
gnaw away at all we see,
while the unseen remains
uncertain and
unfathomable.
All that remains is faith
that hope and love are
enough.

Born Anew

What is it that we await
to be born in us each Christmas day?

We hold our breath in advent's hope
this year will bring the savior home.

Two thousand years of stories told
how can the message not seem old?

What new meaning finds its worth
in retelling the Messiah's birth?

A new star risen in the east
to give hope to the lost and least,

the Word has come to impregnate
every fertile heart by faith

and Mary shows us in due time
we must each give birth to the divine.

Reflecting on Christmas

Before recovery
Christmas was painful.

The coming of the giver of Life
only highlighted
my own self-centeredness.

I hid my face
in a barrel of Whiskey
hoping I would drown,

till one day He came down,
gently lifted my head and said:
I can raise you from the dead.

Do you wish to be made well?

Those words broke
the sodden spell –
shattered

the gates of hell
and I whispered
yes.

Evocation

words
can only convey
so much.

speaking
in symbols and similes
allusions and abstractions

hoping
to evince meaning
from this madness

longing
to draw down the divine
and illumine the mundane.

Longing for the Dawn

dawn breaks but i am not awake
i have become like a nocturnal beast
unable to greet the day

circadian rhythm awry
i watch the stars move across the night sky
and dream of being that early bird

who takes flight at first light
gathering in the sunbeams
and feeling so alive it hurts.

Death in a Box

I am choosing this foolishness
a return to the puissance of adolescence
waste and indolence, cheap rebellion
casting cold embers upon my existence:

a true Fool's folly.

Feeding upon ashes,
ignoring the warnings, defiantly defending
my right to oblivion – oblivious
to the hypocrisy.

no.
that's not quite
right.

Embracing the debasing of my body
is closer to truth, meditating upon
my madness, hiding behind this
smoke screen designed to

block out the feelings, stealing
the moments right out
from under
me.

Dragonflies in Seven Voices

1.

dragonflies!

they fly the skies before your eyes
dipping, twirling – they mesmerize.
iridescent hues of greens and blues
reds, yellows, and oranges too!

today a tiger striped crossed my path
landed nearby and made me laugh.
this summer they showed up everywhere
one even landed in my hair!

2.

other cultures give them a bad rap
"devil's sewing needle' and all that crap
but they eat the bugs that suck my blood
and how can that be anything but good?

3.

tiger stripe came by today
sat on an antennae on a red truck
the wind blew strong, he held on
all four appendages holding fast.

he cocked his head at my approach,
allowing me to wonder at his design.
the wind blew him off once, he came right back;
such determination for no apparent purpose;
was he a messenger? was he a sign?
was he a beautiful she?

no matter, so entranced by the presence
I lost myself for a moment

and wondered aloud:
do insects have feelings just like me?

4.

natives know the message they send
born in water, raised to the sky
two worlds combined in a delicate blend
proof that the old one has to die.

5.

crazy dragonfly big as a tern
dipped at the cars towards the shiny hoods
not quite sure what he was hoping to learn
I guess there's no metal to be found in the woods!

6.

buggy eyed friend, quick as a wink
how can you fly so fast and so high?
playing tag in the marsh with all of your kin
in two short months you have to die.

7.

the season now comes to a close
the autumn leaves are falling fast
just like me, a time to change
for nothing here is bound to last.

circles everywhere I see
nature's way of coming round
the dragonflies, a memory
visceral truth of common ground.

Bird Dance

Eight small birds
swooped and spun
as one

over the still pond

catching bugs
in a perfectly synchronized
spiral dance.

Entrance

On the threshold of decision
>   where the outcome is obscured
faith requires persistence
>   a giving up, a falling in
a commitment to unraveling
>   these layers of defensive gauze
exposing old wounds to the light.

A death, then, of sorts
>   to resurrect the imperishable
and turning inside out
>   choosing to be vulnerable
confronting fear of rejection
>   trusting the invisible
a jumping off the ledge.

Oh spirit indomitable, ineffable, hear me:
>   i have lost my reasoning
all that's left, this hungering
>   after that which i cannot
possibly understand...
>   ...and perhaps that's the plan.

Essence

the heart of wonder
silence

space between moments
eternity

words are symbols, not
truth

perception misperceives
mystery

essence cannot be
conveyed

existence purely
experiential.

Experiential Meditation

A letting go, a soft surrender
allowing thoughts to flow downstream
in this moment all is perfect –
in the gentle glow, touched
by divinity I await
further instruction.

Every muscle relaxed and pliable
the energy flows just where it will
an instrument, a hollow bone –
knowing I am not alone
acquiescing the will to power
becoming calm and still.

Imagine light, my body filled
time no longer has its hold
held by Love's eternal hand –
expectations fall away
unfolding like a flower
which greets the coming day.

For Mary Oliver

twilight silence, frozen pond

sunset mellow orange fades

dotted clouds across horizon

take a dragonesque form

today a Giant passed away

a quiet but insistent voice

reminding us that we belong

wherever we are.

Genuine Artifice

well now

here there is not
the thing which you sought

so by fits and starts
you take it apart

malignant narcissism
your soul's carcinogen

a legacy of divisiveness
and self-serving self-righteousness

will be the only footnote
that history wrote

for king baby.

Hiraeth

A soft rain
gently chides:

stop looking
to externals
for fulfilment.

Wholeness lies
deep within,

Elysian fields
need tending.

Paradise lost
begs to be found

tilling the ground
accepting the cost

not wishing
things to be other
than they are.

Born too early,
or too late –

distinctions are
illusory.

Inherited ideologies
spark separation.

We return home
when we learn to bloom
where we are planted.

Hiraeth (n.) a Welsh word which mean a homesickness for a home to which you cannot return, a home which maybe never was; the nostalgia, the yearning, the grief for the lost places of your past. It is associated with the bittersweet memory of missing something or someone, while being grateful for their existence.

Unbound

All doctrine and dogma aside
the symbol of the Trinity remains inviolate

One God, three distinct persons
endlessly engaging in playful fellowship

Singing universes into existence
inviting all with breath to join the dance:

Ring around the Rosie, pocketful of promise
ashes to ashes, we all fall down –
to rise again.

Ode to Hubris

When I write my magnum opus
let the angels clap their hands
let the heavens bow in wonder
astonished at the power of Man!

God will smile and praise me greatly
proclaim a feast for such a feat
call the masters to the table
Shakespeare, Longfellow, Blake and Keats!

They will ask me how I did it
and I most humbly will proclaim
'tis easy to be named a master
when you judge with your own brain!

Incantation

Ocean, mountain, flowered field
river, canyon, forest wield
wonder under nature's spell
life abounds and all is well.

Desert, fen and frozen waste
quicksand, mudslide, lifeless place
jungles dark and caverns cold
let all nature's truth be told!

There is no light but there be dark
no scrap of death life does not spark
no truth without a hidden clause
no perfect world without its flaws.

Paradox reveals the true
hidden from the common view
woven into space and time
made manifest by simple rhyme!

The Crooked Path to the Light

Atman waits in patient slumber
while all around the senses thunder

the world and its ten thousand things
distract us like bright shiny rings

make us blind to that which matters
leave our soul in hopeless tatters

paupers in the truest sense
acting out this vain pretense

like everything is just okay
while deep inside we waste away

perhaps the path to make us whole
lies in a dark night of the soul.

Invitation for the Soul

Rest here awhile, abide with me
learn to listen with your soul
don't be deceived by what you see
these fragments of a greater Whole.

The walls that you have built are strong
but know that I am stronger still
the day is hard the night is long
there's no such thing as time to kill.

The waiting is the hardest part
the maw of time's infernal beast
gnaws at your bones till you forget
the Sun still rises in the East

and I have come to call you all –
the last the lost the lame the least.

Upwards

Learning to trust is a little like dying,
the hard outer shell cracking
letting in the light.

Vulnerability the only path
to intimacy, the only hope
of becoming alive and connected.

Existence without spirit
is half-life at best,
experience devoid of enthusiasm
is just marking time.

Communication without Love
is merely chatter,
giving without Compassion
an exercise in self-indulgence.

I am guilty of all these faults
and capable of all these aspirations.

On any given day
I will vacillate between the extremes, and
if I am honest and forthright
I will tell you that it is only Grace
that keeps me moving,
however falteringly,
towards the Higher Ground.

Taking Sides

the rhetoric a bottomless pit
in this atmosphere of fear
entrenched in dualistic diatribes
the other becomes the enemy

polarizing attitudes
aggrandize the issues
while media complicity
feeds the hate machine

dehumanization
the decline of western civilization
choking on the bitter fruit
of manifest destiny

it is not too late
is it too late
it is not
is it...

wait. can there be
a true dialogue between the extremes
recognizing the inherent dignity
of every human being?

there is no panacea
that will resolve these dilemmas
no easy road to peace
among the thorns, yet

after exhausting all the words
only one hope remains:
the idea of the other
is no more, leaving only

us.

Serious Advice

If you take yourself too seriously
no one else will

the Sage is the one who embraces
his own foolishness

the World and its ten thousand things
cannot take root

in the fertile soil
of self-deprecating laughter.

On Some Days...

I only want to lay down upon the cool grass
and let my fevered body melt
into the embrace
of the earth.

Blessed forgetfulness, my bones to stones
blood to water, skin become loam,
my organs deposits of
precious minerals.

From dust I have come
and to dust will I return, so may it be
for the good of all.

But I am in no hurry.

As long as wind remains in this temple
so shall I strive for higher things.

And I am not alone.

Ever.

Feelings are not
facts, they are ephemeral

...beneath the surface lies the Real.

Origin

Behind the word you will find the intent

under the intent you will discover the motive

beneath the motive lies the desire

urging the desire is the need

the need arises from the soul

and the soul is always

trying to find its way back

to its Creator.

Petrichor

In this dry season, lightning
flashes without rain, earth
cracks and splits wide open,
entreating the skies
for a modicum
of moisture.

Yearning for rehydration
memory surfaces:
surfeit of water, rippled like
scales of a silver fish, undulating
with the breeze, cool mist
on warm skin.

Parched lips form a rough prayer.
Eyes lifted up, the old one beats the drum.
Feathered bright, donned in turquoise,
now the dance begun, now
the rain will
come.

Quest

Restlessness aside, this day is all I own
to try and piece the mystery
of all that's right in front of me
the passion and calamity
each single heart has known.

Preposterous indeed, to attempt to understand
the music of the spheres
and if god interferes
when the verdict of the years
lies beyond my mortal span.

Indescribable, this joy, that masquerades as pain
the veil of this uncertainty
longing for eternity
deep and wide as any sea
the risk could all be vain.

Ineffable, this grace, which launched a foolish quest
to seek out a connection
between each path's direction
towards the divine reflection
and find my soul at rest.

Roadmap Out of Hell

To look within and own your sin –
your past with all its demons
A fearless search for truth will hurt
but only for a season.

To stay awhile with all the guile
digging though the layers
It may seem vain but from the pain
will blossom earnest prayers.

Beneath the mire your soul respires
despite the suffocation
Dung unearthed will prove its worth
becoming your salvation.

With no regret you place your bet
and sing your darkest song
The truth will out, there is no doubt
you're here where you belong.

Separate No More

Once i thought
i was separate from you
lodged in my story, forging my way

oblivious to the larger life
shackled to my biased perception

like a hungry ghost i wandered
always seeking something
to fill the void.

Futility my monkey
each stone unturned only added
to my onus.

I fed upon wishes and ashes
until i no longer knew
what i wished for

at all.

You came at the darkest hour
my attempted annihilation,
whispered hope and offered me

a thorn.

In my desperation i reached and found
the thorn was a crown
on the rose who arose

and i was no longer

alone.

Servant of Life

O

to be a servant of Life
in a culture of death
this throwaway culture
where every breath
is weighed and measured for usefulness.

AS

it is above, so also below
that which is within, also without
so many things I cannot know
and so I make my peace with doubt
trusting time and Providence will work it out.

I AM

complicit and complacent
with my hands up in the air
this conscience call is nascent
rising from the judgment chair
I thrust these hands into the dirt, sowing Life out there.

Early Morning Rhapsody

Seven crows slide by
a pale sliver of moon –
cawing raucously, awake
to the day's possibilities.

Songbird on the pole
births a rhapsody pure and joyous –
if you listen carefully
it sounds like laughter.

A zephyr wends its way
through the neighborhood trees –
bells chime, leaves swish:
another melodious morning.

Showing Up

We carry this treasure
within us – eternal light
in this fragile vessel

and though our wounds
distinguish us – they do not define
who we are.

Character comes
from deep within – the direct result
of how we live.

We choose to love
despite the pain – showing up for life
again and again.

Snow Drifts

Snow drifts across the frozen lake
thoughts shift forward and back
remembering, hoping, dreaming.
The sun pops out a moment

slips back under cover
wind sighs through the boughs
carry on, carry on
like a mantra it moves me.

The rhythm of my breath a song
gently lilting under heavy skies
bright sun reflected on cold ice
a golden path to the open water.

What lies beneath the frozen crust
circling in the icy depths
life continues unabated
despite empty appearances.

A single goose calls in the distance
no answer but its echo
January rules supreme
its frigid fingers grip the day –

yet somehow hope is born in me
despite the outward gloom
from some secluded room
it has found a way.

The Divine Third

Along the pathway towards Home
there you are, and here am I
but what is that gust of air between us
unseen, but deeply moving?

Just outside my periphery I spy it
like a bright aura around your shadow
living, moving, and having being
animated by our connection.

Wherever two or more are gathered
under the yew tree or in the city
along the riverbank and in the tenements
every conversation is a testament

revealing the power of the Word.

Flow of the Universe

All this noise
the silence is buried
in a parallel dimension
behind the vibrations
awaiting discovery

All this time
the present is missing
swallowed by illusion
days of future passed
all unredeemable

All this turmoil
peace lies dormant
underneath the busyness
anesthetization embraced
illegitimate substitute

Meanwhile, the universe
like a river, unhurried,
unfolding as it flows,
embracing all in its path,
anticipates our awakening.

Where the Trouble Lies

The head is where the trouble lies
    incessant thoughts which manifest
and buzz around like swarms of flies
    I chase and swat and get no rest

I guess it should be no surprise
    this heavy feeling in my chest
if the heart is where the treasure lies
    it is buried under mounds of stress.

Poet's Calling

I need to write, yet inspiration
sometimes lacks imagination

And so I toss a heap of words
out on the page, which sound absurd

In hopes that some will fall in place:
a poet's stab at saving face.

I circle back where I began,
bereft of feeling, yet still a man

Who seeks to say what must be said
to break the rules and wake the dead.

Wheel Turns

The wheel turns, stars
fade in and out of view
life begins and ends every moment.

The wren sings and the Jackdaw croaks,
children laugh and the tribes of the world
play capture the flag.

At the center of the wheel is the stillness
largely unnoticed by the busy throng
untouched by the vicissitudes of time
inaccessible through commerce or coercion
unknowable by philosophy or dogma or reason
yet infinitely present
in each fragile breath.

Trade winds blow across the globe
empires rise and fall, still
the center of the wheel
remains unchanged
impervious to manipulation
undaunted and ineffable.

The sea swells and recedes
while the sun makes its rounds
and the moon drives us to madness with its beauty
all things bright and beautiful
merely reflections
of that sacred stillness.

Time Moves

Time moves as I type these words
slowly beating out the measure of my life
my hand can no longer hold the pen and
I cannot remember life without pain.

This is no exercise in self pity nor
sorrow at what might have been –
this is an assemblance of the facts
a stab at objectivity.

In the middle portion of my life
(one can never be quite sure)
I have seen my own darkness turned inside out
exposed to the light and negated

yet the shadows remain.
I see your wounds,
share your humanity
yet still I would judge you with my lesser self.

We who are so fond of labels
would see the world in black and white
each soul neatly boxed and shelved:
everything in its right place.

God too is placed in a box
(albeit a larger one with brighter colors)
placed on the altar of our own understanding
worshipped in our own accustomed style.

We fear the others
who question the box
never comprehending
we have boxed in ourselves

and so the divine
eludes our grasp
and all the boxes
remain empty.

Metamorphosis

i have known
since i was twelve
that i was a poet

the first poem
i ever wrote
did not rhyme

what a lot
of crap
i took for that

clever boy that i was
i immersed myself in rhyme
until i could do it all the time

inspirational lyrical poetry
and it was good
as far as it went

i even heard once
a nun was using it
during her devotional time

and it sounds lovely
when read aloud
in a room full of devotees

but the heart has left it;
and so it remains
a shining monument

an intentional offering
of all the things i thought
that i should be.

Upon the Turning

Five hawks circling over water
wind holding its breath
against the panoply of a clear blue sky
I contemplate my death.

Verdant fields have rusted brown
shrouded with the fallen leaves
autumn's change made manifest
as the ghosts of summer grieve.

And I must change like all the rest
sloughing off my coarse array
as all creation will attest
the old must pass away.

Warning Global Warming

If you go

ice fishing in March

don't blame the pond

if it swallows you whole.

Dynamism

World spins, mind turns
problems rise, give way, and fall
wind blows, soul yearns
to join the One behind it all.

Dharma, karma, reap and sow
all universal laws apply
these shadows here are all I know
yet cling to all that passes by

Still, this hope will not be quelled
release from time's entropic grip
once this earthly husk is shelled
all the puzzle pieces fit.

44 Selected Poems

The Will of God Is Like a River

The will of God is like a River
      rolling towards a mighty Sea
I try to calm myself to feel it
      and let the waters set me free.

The River flows with grace and mercy
      the waters roil with vibrancy
I stand upon the Shore and marvel
      that such an offer comes to me.

The River runs with wild abandon
      the waves explode in ecstasy
Who can staunch this mighty concourse
      the rush of those the Son sets free.

O mighty River I beseech you
      take me now against my will
Sweep me in Your arms of plenty
      till all the sodden earth be stilled.

I stand upon the edge of nothing
      looking, longing for the Real
The barren wasteland weighs my feet down
      soul and spirit both to steal.

River! River! I implore you
      rise strong and wild to pull me in
Drown me in your effervescence
      that the true Life may begin!

The Sacred Dance

If I turn to hear the wind
and let the sacred dance begin
all that binds me to this earth
reveals itself of little worth.

For all that is has been before
and all that was will be again
the dance transcends this earthen floor
we step in time with our True friend
who leads us straight to heaven's door
in our beginning is our end.

O glorious and blessed Peace
is there a way to find release?

It's all I have that keeps me poor
and all I need that draws me near
the wolf is howling at the door
I only feed him out of fear
for holy poverty ignores
the locust who devours the years.

The attachment brings the suffering
we are in chains to what we cling
the Master comes, we are set free
and learn to dance synchronously.

A Poet Lost In the Wilderness

Ah, the blessed forest
where the green wildness
beckons me home, like a primordial paradise.

Yet, here I am
in this forlorn structure of concrete and steel
wasting away, and pining for something more.

I have found myself, like Dante,
in the midway of my life astray
at a loss for the Straight way.

In here, the sounds of business
clog the spirit, and the busy-ness
make all my choices seem the same.

There have been moments of gratitude,
instants of forgetfulness
in this shallow wilderness,

where I have had acceptance
and been attentive to the lessons
taught through loss and rejection.

There have been tiny victories –
though mostly over insecurities –
and altogether few and far between.

Ah, once again I digress
and find the pain of loneliness
in every breath.

The chasm between the ideals of youth
and the realities of age widens
as I struggle to keep family afloat.

O, to be here now; here,
at the intersection of the eternal and the temporal
to see things as they really are, now:

to behold the Divine presence here
underneath the papers and reports
in the voice of all who call for answer

the Creator speaking, softly, ever present
beneath every frustration, behind
every supposed failure.

The holiness is in the doing, the sacred space
the place in which I choose to make
my moments matter.

I look for revelations in the form of open doors
instead of looking for the doors which open
in your eyes, and in your soul.

I listen to the dull sound of the clicking keys
and the drone of the fan, and forget
the music of the heart.

Awake! The time is now, the hour already late!
No time to waste in wishing or wanting
that which cannot satisfy the longing.

The Static Hub of the Whirling Universe

Beyond the words
Behind the reason
Under the veneer of the changing seasons

Between the atoms
Beneath the stars
Behold! The universe is ours

In every breath
On every tongue
The song of Creation longs to be sung

Above all else
Before all time
We await the fullness of the divine

To see the truth
To feel the real
To know the whole
Which will reveal

The holy whisper
That noise inters
Deep in the dark
Below the words

The sacred image
Perfect, remains
The mystery
Begins again

All that is reminds us
All that was behind us
All that will be binds us
To us
To us.

The Heart Of God

The heart of God
a child's smile
often passes us right by, as we
scurry off to keep some deadline
somewhere, in some predetermined time
taking for granted
all that's been granted
missing the point
entirely.

Tidal Pull

sadness ebbs, the soul's unsteady
wreckage in the wake of wrath
lonely echoes, like the seashell
reverberate the aftermath

thoughts are caught in tidal pools
swirling with the rhythmic sea
looking for the inlet out
to catch the flow and be set free

trying hard to ride the waves
toward the shelter of the shore
will I ever find my neap tide or
will I always long for more?

In Cold Seasons of Self

I

It amazes me, Your patience
In times of trouble, seasons of doubt
Embedded in my anger
Searching for understanding
I forget what you are all about.

II

Could I, in bondage to abstract reason
Deny You, engaged in mental treason
I stumble, waiting for the words I
Fumble into the absurd.

III

A prefabricated defense?
An elaborate pretense?
Can I refute the obvious fact
I'm keeping my pride intact.
A misguided rationalization?
A ruse of my own creation?
Shall I succumb to mere temptation
A demonstration of demoralization
Of hard luck stories and allegories
Degenerating into
An avoidance of the issue
At hand.

IV

And can I deny the sin within
Giving in to every whim
Clinging to Your grace
As an excuse for being base?

V

O Lord, forgive my trepidation
These anxious thoughts that overwhelm
When I'm distressed by situation, please
Remind me that You're at the helm.hat You're at the helm.

Purposelessness

I have stood on the edge
felt the thrum of the continuum
as the universal energy passed by –
connections made and lost and
reformed, creating new patterns of light.

Where do I fit in? How do I
dive in? Where is my
purpose?

Waiting wishing wondering why
all this time goes sailing by
leaving nothing in its wake
except the road I did not take.

Archetypical Madness

lover
trickster
warrior
king

we're each
a bit
of
everything

and when
we leave
our hearth
and kin

to sail
alone,
we soon
begin

to find
the depths
we can
assail

and lose
ourselves
to seek
the Grail.

Damn the Histrionics

Sometimes it all gets too intense
and I will try and hide away
behind a wall of great defense
the battlements of yesterday.

    Summoning my will to act
    I cannot see that which I lack
    and if, perchance, I should look back
    what will be my legacy?

If indeed my words ring true
and there is nothing left to fear
would it be the same with you
if I chance to let you near?

    Will I see you as you are,
    or as you wish to be revealed?
    Can I convey my soul's malaise,
    and trust your lips will remain sealed?

Enigma

Emotions rise and fall like the tides, and I
have learned the art of riding them
to some extent;

and although I am not
under the waves, there are still times where
I am barely treading water.

Feelings flowing freely, flowing faster, knowing
nothing lasts forever, feelings passing, hoping
to fix my eyes upon the eternal, trying

to keep my footing while
the maelstrom
rages on.

O for the peace, the peace which passes
all understanding – the world cannot know it, nor
remove it from one's soul.

God's peace, that blessed cessation
of againstness awaits me at the point
of letting go.

In The Face of All Aridity

I long for more than what I am,
I linger long in speculation
Digging in now with both hands
Shaking off the long stagnation

The unearthed soil, pungent and repugnant –
The soul recoils and seeks escape in a thousand
Diversions, echoes of each rationalization
Reverberate within the fallow ground –

Heaven's lost and found.

Here lies the valley of the shadow.
        The darkness buried deep, the Shade
Behind every good intention, awaiting
        A weaker moment to arise.

Letting Go

sometimes I feel so inadequate.

the words come, slow and
labored and I strain to explain
but somehow fall
short of
cohesion.

how can I give myself, complete,
without holding back
and not feel the pain
and loss of this
abandon?

ah God, here I am balking at every turn,
a child who can't let go
clinging to my possessions, unmindful
that they are possessing
me.

Depth

The Love of God is like an ocean
Strong and Deep and Wide and Wild
Our heart's call is to devotion
To learn to love Him as a child

Bittersweet are start and ending
Now old is what was once called new
Our will grown supple from the bending
We learn to live our life anew

Every heartache will be transformed
Changed by grace to precious stones
Worn by those that love has conformed
Into the image of His own.

Soulmate (for Krissy)

I tried to find
the noblest way
to speak my heart –
for all you are
and all you do
continues to
amaze me.

Life is changing
once again
it seems we wake
and never stop
till sleep descends
and then we wake
to try again.

I will not lose
your heart in all
this busy-ness.

I do not know
where we would be
without each other
to have and hold
richer or poorer –
often poorer in riches
but richer in graces
in sickness and health
holding hands –
the comfort of embraces.

We have learned
that God is faithful
even when
we forget.

I love you with

all I have
all I am
all I hope to be,
our children are
so very blessed
in every way,
and every day
they reflect
the love we share.

Our lives in flux
do not allow
discouragement
a foothold, or
disheartenment
to close a door.

I love you more
each moment spent
our hearts entwined
with contentment
there is no past
we should lament
trials forge the heart
with strong cement
I know our love
is heaven sent
and we'll grow old
beautifully bent
in to the earth
our clay's descent
our spirits soar:
heaven's ascent.

That Inescapable Anger

Rising up it grabs me by the throat and
makes me into what I loathe –
this fury takes me where
I fear to go.

Under layers of morbid thought
I sought to bury that which lingers,
ever a weight around my neck,
never quite released from its fetid grip.

And at times it will arise and block
all semblance of reason moving my
will towards that which is base – this madness, reeking of
self-pity and longing to exert some force

by which my perceived powerlessness
may be eradicated, attempting to
reverse the cycle of shame
and remorse by force.

Forgive me, my Lord.
Please forgive me and remember,
I am made of dust

Wake

the cars lined up in
the glistening sunlight
the men in their pressed black suits and
their courteous expressions welcome
my wife and i into the home.

there is a box at the altar, just behind
the prie-deiu
with his name inscribed in gold
lettering.

i kneel and ask mercy
on his soul and
my own and
peace for his family
left behind.

the reality of the loss
begins to draw me out of myself
and i am present, knowing
this is where i need to be.

Sacred Circle

Set apart and sanctified, this other world
with all its primal flavor and colorings
and reminders of who we really are
beneath the surface.

Naked in spirit
we return to this First world,
to feed our hunger for Truth and
slake our thirst for silence
from the wellspring of our ritual.

In the sanctuary of the Circle,
we lay bare our secret hearts
and unearth those insecurities
unfamiliar to that second world, the world
of illusion by which we know so little
and are so little known.

We descend
into the realm of our original selves
the rhythm we engender replicates
the earth's own heartbeat
our inherent separation melts away
as we partake in
the great Mystery of creation.

Black and White

In days of old, the knights came round
To slay the wicked dragons down
The captives freed, the maidens fair
Would sing their praises everywhere

They'd feast on meat and wine and bread
And toast the awful Dragon's head
Then off to dream about the Grail
They'd wake the morning, setting sail

The knights are gone, their legends left
Within our hearts, yet sore bereft
Are we who struggle with our plight
To see the world in black and white.

On the Precipice

The way is long, the path grows steep
where darkness gathers in the deep
yet we are children, born to light
we fear no shadows of the night.

Though many hours before we sleep
with constant vigilance we keep
the narrow path which leads the way
through Shadow's heart to greet the Day.

We do not walk this road alone
we give each other's heart a home
each burden borne, a lighter soul
and one step closer to the Whole.

Alienation

It's funny how
It seems to be
That you're like you
And I'm like me
And that there is
No in-between
Or at least
That's what it seems.

Can we look
Beyond the guise
And seek the truth
Behind the lies
Perhaps in time
We both will see
I'm quite like you
And you, like me.

Acceptance

Acceptance brings
The sweet release
That hate denied
And grants us peace
To face ourselves
Our pride aside
To give the love
We were denied.

Wisdom's task
To show the way
When darkness shrouds
And doubt decays
To let us know
That feelings pass
Faith, hope, and love
Are all that last.

Joy will come
And pierce the pain
Letting life
Come through again
Bringing truth
To all our sorrows
Exchanging despair
For bright tomorrows.

The table placed
In pastures green
A banquet set
A lover's dream
The calling comes
For all who hear:
Accept the gift
Refuse the fear.

Not Here

i am not here,
not
in the moment.

the mind stretching out
beyond the present
tries to claw its way
into the future.

all this worry:

pointless.

Hope

all in, the world's gone mad
   my eyes are bleeding from the bad
   that people do in lieu of thinking
   god is blind and satan's winking
    doubletalk and single file
     substance gone to worship style
      eating crap the media feeds
       sowing death with every seed
        insanity the soup du jour
         the masses long for something more
         underneath the sheer veneer
        buried beneath piles of fear
       the core remains untouched by hate
      and issues multifoliate
     the tree of life is still in bloom
    it's just in some other room
   right beyond the chamber door
is the place we will find More.

I Scream Inside

all this virtual nonsense, this literal
alienation drives me out of
my mind. nothing comes
from nothing – I spend my days
typing, typing, typing, answering the
phone when it rings, still no
real communication here, just
the facts, ma'am, just
the facts.

I feel my spirit crushed within me, I cannot
pretend that this is satisfying anymore, I long
to bolt right out the door and return
nevermore.

nevermore to hear the sterile sounds of the keys pounded in haste
to rush and get the next thing done so the next thing can be done. it
never ends, there is no end of busyness
in business.

I want to jump up on my desk and scream over
the silly cubicle wall, "This is not me, this happy idiot
struggling for the legal tender, this is just a shell
occupying a seat for seven point seven five hours a day, this is not
me, this is not my life, this is not…"

…going to happen of course, but at least i can smile
at the thought of rebelling against the chains of responsibility that
have held me fast for so long.

so,
help me
God.

More

i wanted

to talk about

my favorite obsession

but i could not

choose

just one.

Stuck

it is time now
to look forward. no more
clinging to the rotted stumps
of yesterday's blooms.

the morass is thick, regrets choke
the tender shoots of tomorrow's fruits
blunders made, it's all smoke
to blind my eyes, forget my roots.

it is now time
to live forward. no more
pathetic askance glances
at what might have been.

i am no martyr, no blessed Mahatma
surrender tears me to the core
all things change, my soul grows faint
must i always long for more?

The God Who Hides

The natives looked
for lessons under
every leaf and rock – they knew
you were a God who likes to hide.

We build cathedrals, paint them
immaculate and fill them
with statues, icons, and other accoutrements –
effectively hiding God.

I went for a walk
and sat by a brook, and that
is where I heard
You laughing.

The Space In-Between

here
in this space –
between
the knowing
and the
longing

lies the uncertainty
of no rituals;
the discomfort
of displacement.

always searching,
r e a c h i n g
for that
higher ground.

why bother
when the truth is

grace
      flows
            down.

Damsel in Distress

I remember
when I was younger
I wanted to be
the knight in
shining armor.

I would rescue
every maiden
from their dragon.

I would release
all the prisoners
from their unjust chains.

I would ride in
on my white horse
and save the day.

How disconcerting
to find out
I was
actually
the
damsel
in distress
all along.

A Plant Growing from Under a Rock
(Sometimes I Feel Like)

the rock is heavy.
this bloom is fragile, yet
determined.

the sky looms bright, promising
sunlight, heat and
growth.

unable to grow upwards,
sideways will have to
suffice.

the One who
made the flower
is well acquainted
with the rock,
after
all.

Manifesto

i will not force my way
i will not break the door
i will not clench my fists
i will not wage this war

i will no longer suffer
i will no longer fear
i will no longer take the reins
i will no longer steer

i will not linger loudly
i will not shout complaint
i will not curse the heavens
i will not lack restraint

i will surrender willingly
i will my will retire
i will embrace a life of grace
i will walk on sacred Fire

i will now kiss the present
i will now free the past
i will now hope for future
i will now make Now last

i will give to all who ask me
i will make no more demands
i will tend to my own garden
i will walk in fertile lands.

It Is What It Is
(for Dad)

It is what it is
      the old man would say,
why ruffle your feathers
      and get in the way?

God has a plan
      though he didn't tell you
or check with you first
      to make sure what to do

Why hold on so tightly?
      why make such a fuss?
let go of the past
      make a gesture of trust

Stop running around
      trying to fix all the holes
let the rain come in gently
      and clean out your soul

Stop hiding your troubles
      quit stuffing your fears,
God already knows them
      let him wipe your tears

You know, it is what it is
      the old man would say
and I can still hear him speak
      when I get out of the way.

I Am No Mystic

I am no mystic,
no sublime saint –
though my thoughts
are often set above

it is here and now
the proving ground –
to act in haste
or chose to love?

There are no answers,
only questions –
framed in theological
debates, yet

when I let go
of these abstractions –
the peace that descends
is worth the wait.

Roadmap

As i travel
this long road
i am not alone.

The signposts placed
by those who went before
direct me towards a bright horizon.

Their stories provide
a roadmap across the barren wilderness
and each meeting, a filling station for the soul.

Stars (5-7-5)

At night, beneath stars
all the world seems still and cold
while the earth awaits

the morning's rebirth.
Awaiting revelation
all creation sings.

So cold, they appear
silver sparkling silhouettes
set on ebony,

infinite in space.
No man can count the number,
yet God knows their names.

Indescribable
lost in absolute wonder
words cannot express.

The stars are constant:
even when we cannot see,
they shine just as bright.

Waking Up

Eyes closed,
breathe deep into
being: be here,
truly here.

Prickling skin
reveals aliveness,
a witness to
existence.

Slow breathing
the anchor
forcing attention
into bodily sensations.

The deeper self
forcing its way up.

Perception altered,
only the present remains.

A Lesson from the Elements

1. earth

rich pungent smell of old life decayed
the soil brings forth the naked truth
memories of what once was displayed

in earthen form, raw and uncouth.
All life will pass in likewise way
discarding the old in favor of youth;

Gaia embraces the funeral display
takes the shell while the soul departs
Hemera burns bright another day

here ends earth where water starts.

2. water

drip drop drop drop drip

deluge brought up the sunken ship
up from depths of deepest dark
into the light the shadow slips
the broken hull, sullen and stark
waterlogged and rife with rot

drop drip drip drip drop

3. air

wind echoes in the caverns
stirring up dust, the same dust
we are made of;

i breathe in the atmosphere
consciously integrating

this simple truth:

life is sacred, the spirit
that God has given to us
bears this witness.

4. fire

cleansing, purging, warming, lighting
untamed, raw, a little frightening

dancing, burning, raging, flaring
under stars our secrets sharing

scorching, molding, charring, healing
thank Prometheus for stealing!

5. void

between the emptiness

and the form

behind the obvious

of the norm

lies the no-thing.

Trust

If I am really trusting You
my fear will vanish
like the morning dew

Once I have learned to let it go
anxiety will melt
like the April snow

When I begin surrendering
grace will flow
like a river in spring

If I will heed Your gentle call
I will learn to dance
like a leaf in fall

All these things I long to be
all these things I already am
perfected in the eyes of God
it is only me that I will damn.

Evergreen

Even when death is all around
Even when truth cannot be found
When all life is underground
Evergreen, ever green.

Clearer than a mountain stream
Lovelier than a lover's dream
Straight and tall, wild and clean
Come with me, ever green.

Other trees, our fellows true
Bloom in every shape and hue
All equal in Creator's view
We are one, ever green

When the leaves have all gone brown
Pine cones rotting all around
A sprig of green comes from the ground
Nothing dies, ever green.

Resonance

The bells, the bells
 they toll and keen
They shatter peace
 for those who dream
Of better life –
 the other side
 The bells, they wail
we run and hide.

The gulls, they whirl
 in spiral dance
We hear their cries
 as in a trance
Lie on the shore
 and wait for fate
To lead the way
 to something great.

Smoke ascends
 the river flows
Earth is hard
 and fire glows
Man will cling
 to what has passed
Time sands shift
 he fails to grasp.

The bells
they ring
the gulls
they sing
The sand
it drifts
the river
shifts...

Making waves upon the ocean
rolling out into the sea
the river keeps the sand in motion
beckoning eternity...

...becoming to...
...coming to...
...come to...
...come...

In Medias Res
(into the middle of things)

All life begins in media res.

We are always in the middle of a death
or birth, dirge or ode, spate or
dearth; existence is, and we
simply are.

A soul has no definitive
origin, each life has no particular
end, then again:
the seed of ending is sown in each beginning.

How could it be otherwise?

We think we can put god in a box, squeeze
the universe into a ball, place
existence under a
microscope...

but –

God doesn't stay in the box, the
universe continually expands, and
existence is multidimensional.

Here, in the middle of things, always
today, the very life of life flowers and
grows, ebbs and flows, leaving us
breathless and longing, seeking
meaning – dreaming, always
dreaming, hoping for,
longing for,
more.

Grief's Grey Grip

The pain, exhausting.
what words are left cannot convey
the loss. this agony stretches out
across the span of time, the days
flow ever on and still the aching
hole remains.

I try to turn to God, I know
in peaceful sleep he let her go
no suffering, no prolonged pain
to leave behind a darkened stain
upon our memories so bright
and though, a time, beyond our sight
forever in my soul, remain
until that day we meet again.

Hope does not disappoint, and yet
so weary, so world worn, I wish to lie
down upon the earth, my mother
let the green grass embrace my form
till there is no separation
between what there is
and what was
here now,
here
in depth
arising once again
shaking off the ashes
lifting up my eyes, calling
for the One who resurrects me.

Still and all the feelings rage
up and down across the page
still at once, too soon ablaze
anger melts to cold blasé

underneath the deepest blue
I hear despair come calling too
until I yield my whole estate
I am so grateful that You wait.

Mom
3/8/43 – 10/5/08

too young, alas
without warning you left us
no time for sad farewells
no soft caress, save the one
left as your body cooled
in the hospital bed.

so peaceful, you left us
an image of placidity, your visage
etched in golden pallor
there upon the sacred bier.

no long goodbyes, no anguished cries
you drifted off into that long good-night.

I imagined
His hand reaching down to take yours
leading you Home.

Robert Eugene Perry is a native of Massachusetts. He has crafted poetry since the age of twelve. After many youthful indiscretions and travels across the U.S. to find meaning in his life, he returned to his home state and discovered what it means to bloom where you are planted.

In 2007 he self-published his first novel Where the Journey Takes You, a spiritual allegory which combined poetry and prose to elucidate the concept of life as a journey. This was followed by a collection of poetry The Sacred Dance: Poetry to Nourish the Spirit in 2008.

His second novel Compassion in the Wasteland, was published in 2010, also combining poetry and prose. The story intertwines the lives of various individuals using the Fisher King motif, showing how we are all connected. This was followed by the poetry collection If Only I Were a Mystic, This Would All Come So Easy in 2011.

Perry hosted a poetry group for disabled individuals at the former New England Dream Center in Worcester MA, and has emceed the monthly Open Mic at Booklovers' Gourmet in Webster MA since May 2017.

Two of Perry's poems have been accepted for Poetica Magazine's upcoming 2020 Mizmor Anthology regarding spirituality and nature: "The Divine Third" and "Snow Drifts. His poem "Quest" was the January 2019 Poets of Mars winner.

A self-styled metaphysical poet, he draws inspiration from nature and endeavors to draw connections between our higher selves and the natural world. He is a devoted husband and father of two grown boys.

"The link between the ordinary and the divine is the stuff of Robert Perry's poems, and readers will have no trouble experiencing his vision. Commerce and daily life swirl around us while the eternal center holds, and Perry relishes our fragility as "the moon drives us to madness with its beauty"…while we seek that "sacred stillness.""

Karen Warinsky, author of Gold in Autumn

"To read the poetry of Robert Eugene Perry, well-crafted verse filled with astute observations of both the natural and spiritual world, is to accompany the author on a journey of often profound yet joyous contemplation on his way to personal (and universal) enlightenment."

Paul Szlosek, Co-Founder and Co-Host of the Poetorium at Starlite

"This book is delightful. Robert has an ability to weave eclectic words into many different types of poetry yet they complement each other. I judge poetry by the emotions it brings into my awareness so it is very much a journey through a realm that is fresh and relevant."

Deborah Korch Clinical Reflexologist, Yoga Therapist, Certified Alcohol and Drug Counselor (CADC)

"With his affinity for the spiritual and for nature, Robert's poetry provides another way to explore and understand our world, touching on both singular and universal truths. His words, his poems, with elements of faith and hope and observations of nature are a welcome respite from the ordinary."

Robin Ballou Boucher, Treasurer, Worcester County Poetry Association

"Robert's poetry breathes with the sense of one who has found peace amongst turmoil. His hard earned wisdom and sense of the calm after the storm, is bestowed upon all who surrender to the path."

Tianna Mercier~ Fellow Poet and EFT Practitioner

Made in the USA
Middletown, DE
05 July 2020